To:

/

From:

WHAT I WOULD TELL
MY YOUNGER SELF

by Kylie Johnson

This book is dedicated to my daughter Jazzy
and her future adult self.

Giving thanks to my Grandma Mardy, mum,
dad, sisters, daughter and every single person
that has crossed my path to inspire me and
teach all the lessons I needed.

First published in 2024 by New Holland Publishers
Sydney

Level 1, 178 Fox Valley Road, Wahroonga, NSW 2076, Australia

newhollandpublishers.com

Copyright © 2024 New Holland Publishers
Copyright © 2024 in text and images: Kylie Johnson

A record of this book is held at the National Library of Australia.

ISBN 9781760796662

Managing Director: Fiona Schultz
Designer: Kylie Johnson
Production Director: Arlene Gippert
Printed in China

10 9 8 7 6 5 4 3 2 1

Keep up with New Holland Publishers:

 NewHollandPublishers

 @newhollandpublishers

INTRODUCTION

This little book of Super Powers will help you to find the magic within and live the life you deserve.

Start each day in a Happy Way!

Take a trip with Wise Whiskers the bunny, as she shares her wisdom from the past to her younger self. She helps you to embrace life's wonders and challenges with courage, kindness, and love on your journey to growing up!

This is your little book of life tips.
So you can BE all that you want to be…
DO all that you want to do… and
HAVE all that you hope to have.

CONTENTS

LOVE IS MY SUPER POWER
Love Conquers All
Start each day in a loving way...

When we truly love ourselves and accept who we are, we can give, receive, and feel love more easily. When we believe in our own value and worth and have self-love, it is like wearing a powerful cape that helps us set clear rules on how others should treat us. This helps us attract more kind and caring people into our lives, so love what you do, love who you are and treat everyone with equal love. Always remember that nobody is perfect, however, when we view others through a lens of love and forgiveness, we appreciate their unique and loveable imperfections. Showing love through kindness, thoughtfulness and affection is what makes the world a happier place. Love surrounds you and can be found in family, friendships, relationships, animals, mother nature and all the things that bring you joy! To love and to be loved, is all you need.

POSITIVITY IS MY SUPER POWER
Find the positive side

Start each day in a happy way...

Always try and find the good in everything, even if it takes a little effort sometimes. When you face challenges, see them as chances to grow and learn. Your positive energy is like a contagious good vibe, so share it with everyone around you.

Enter the room with the positive energy you wish to receive.

It is super important to be mindful of any negative thoughts and words as they have more power than you think.

Your happiness depends on the quality of your thoughts and words; what you say and think can affect your mood and experiences so always speak kindly about yourself and others.

Think of it in terms of negative attracts more negative and positive attracts more positive vibes. Choosing to be positive is actually a skill that you can learn and practice. So choose to replace negative self-talk with more encouraging and kind words, so you can live the life of your dreams. Retrain your brain to see the glass as half full and not half empty. Focus on the good and not the bad!

MINDFULNESS IS MY SUPER POWER

Be mindfully present to your feelings, surroundings and actions

Start each day in a mindful way...

Being mindful means paying attention to your thoughts and feelings and everything around you. Mindfulness is noticing what you see, smell, taste, hear and feel. Embrace all of your senses and appreciate the beauty around you. Taking a walk in nature and noticing all of your surroundings helps you let go of any worries and calms your mind.

To find peace take deep breaths outdoors to reset your mood. Worrying about the past or future can lead to anxiety, stress, and sadness. Always remember that true happiness comes from being mindful of our thoughts and surroundings and staying present in each moment.

If you catch yourself worrying, try to bring yourself back to the present of where you are and let go of trying to control any outcomes.

When you are more self-aware you can take better control of your emotions and actions and make better choices. Mindfulness is also taking a moment to think before you speak which helps you respond calmly in any situation.

Find your happy place through a mindfulness activity, whether it is painting, drawing, cooking, gardening, building, designing, crafting, or playing sports, do more of what makes you feel you are escaping in a creative flow, leaving any worries behind.

GRATITUDE IS MY SUPER POWER

Keep an attitude of gratitude

Start each day in a grateful way...

Try to make gratitude a daily habit in your life. Thinking about the things you already have can make you feel happier, however, if you focus on things you don't have , it may bring you down and make you feel bad.

Being grateful can lift your mood and attract more good things into your life, therefore notice and appreciate all the little things you already have.

However focusing on what you think you lack can often leave you feeling unmotivated and sad. Instead compare yourself to those who have less than you and you will soon see there's much to be thankful for in your life.

It is like magic, when you are grateful more good things tend to show up. An attitude of gratitude is like a miracle attractor. Successful people train their minds to be thankful and keep gratitude practices such as journals, gratitude jars and daily prayers.

When you catch yourself focusing on what you do not have, notice how it affects your mood. Remember, gratitude is the most important attitude to stay happy.

Do not forget that saying thank-you is also good manners which makes people feel appreciated and want to do more for you.

A grateful heart is a loved heart.

KINDNESS IS MY SUPER POWER

Spread kindness like confetti

Start each day in a kind way...

A kind heart is a beautiful heart. When you show kindness you will also receive kindness.

Kindness can be felt through being gentle, thoughtful, compassionate and understanding.

Never let anyone's unkindness bring you down, especially bullies. Treat others the way you want to be treated and hold your kindness power by staying calm, strong, and gentle. Being kind can make bullies realise their actions are not okay.

It takes two unkind people to keep a fight on-going. Be the bigger person and show kindness by example. Every act of kindness makes the world a more loving place. A small act of kindness can give someone strength, change their mood, or give hope when they need it most.

You never know what a person is going through, so let your smile of kindness brighten their day. Being kind is cool because kindness always wins! Spreading kindness brings good feelings and the universe rewards you in mysterious ways.

SELF LOVE IS MY SUPER POWER

Happiness starts with self love

Start each day in a loving way....

Taking care of yourself and staying true to your values is part of self-care. Self-love means putting yourself first and setting clear boundaries to protect yourself. A happy and confident person takes care of themselves first so they can be strong enough to care for others.

When you love yourself, you attract kind people into your life. It is okay to say no gently as it means you are taking care of yourself and you do not need to prove anything.

Remember, you cannot help others if you are not okay yourself, so take care of your own needs first. Self-love is not selfish but rather essential for your well-being.

Do more of the things that make you happy and less of what does not. Find your happy place and go there whenever you feel sad or unmotivated.

BELIEVING IS MY SUPER POWER
Believe in yourself and you will be unstoppable
Start each day in a believing way...

Your thoughts have a big impact on how happy and successful you can be in life. It is like magic, what you think about yourself, you become. And when you speak and think positively about yourself, more good things come your way.

Remember, no one knows your dreams better than you do. We are all born with our own special dreams and wishes and sometimes family and friends do not always know and understand what your heart whispers to you. That is okay, only you know what you are capable of achieving.

It can be tough sometimes because doubts may try and stop you, but do not let them! Keep believing in yourself and keep going. When you speak about your dreams as if they are already happening, it is like a sprinkle of magic making them come true, little by little.

Dreams may take time and hard work so follow your heart and anything can happen. Even if you do not achieve your biggest dream, always remain open to unexpected opportunities that may lead you to new and exciting places.

Believe in yourself, no matter what! Shoot for the moon, even if you miss, you will land among the stars.

DETERMINATION IS MY SUPER POWER

Determination is passion in action

Start each day in a determined way...

Having determination means your heart is truly in it and think of your heart as a compass guiding your passion.

Do not worry about facing challenges or obstacles, determination will help you overcome them. Keep moving forward because that is how you grow!

Take small steps towards your goals every day and visualise clearly where you want to be.

With lots of effort you can achieve anything you set your mind to.

A determined spirit helps you achieve great things.

FRIENDLINESS IS MY SUPER POWER

Treasure good friendships

Start each day in a friendly way...

It is important to be careful in choosing your close group of friends because "your tribe becomes your vibe." Surround yourself with friends who have similar values and beliefs as you do as they can really shape who you become and influence your decisions.

A true friend is someone you can trust and rely on, no matter what. They stick with you through the good times and the tough times.

Being popular or having lots of friends is not the most important thing in life, what truly matters is having quality friends who care about you and support you.

Embrace your fun side, your quirks and uniqueness and you will attract the right friends who appreciate you for who you are. When you show compassion, thoughtfulness and kindness, you naturally attract good friendships. A good friend is one that is honest, cares, listens and shows empathy.

Just be yourself and the right friends will come into your life. Stay true to who you are and you will find amazing friends who love you for being you.

FORGIVING IS MY SUPER POWER
A forgiving heart is a healed heart
Start each day in a forgiving way...

A forgiving person is strong and confident. Forgiving others sets you free from pain and anger. Staying angry is like drinking poison and expecting the other person to suffer.

Apologising first, shows maturity and strength and melts away any bad feelings or anger.

It is important to let emotions settle and then communicate gently without too much time passing.

Forgiving and saying sorry is like a magic medicine that heals hurt feelings. Forgiving does not mean you accept bad behaviour, it just sets you free from pain or holding any grudges.

Life is too short to stay mad, so learn to forgive, let it go and move forward.

COURAGE IS MY SUPER POWER

Courage takes you to exciting places

Start each day in a courageous way...

Having courage is like having a magical key that opens the door to new and exciting places. If we do not have courage, we miss out on many wonderful opportunities. If you always do the same things, you will always get the same results, however, if you think outside the box and take a leap of faith to try new things, amazing adventures await you!

Being brave and taking action to do challenging things is the way we grow confidence, so do not let fear be the boss of you! Face your fears, be brave and push through those uncomfortable feelings. You will feel amazing and super proud of yourself afterwards!

Choosing courage over comfort is the only way to grow and achieve big dreams.

CREATIVITY IS MY SUPER POWER
Find your creative outlet
Start each day in a creative way...

Discover your preferred way of being creative and make it your special happy place. When we engage in creative activities we can lose track of time, let go of any worries and feel more calm. Being creative is like doing a special type of meditation that can make us feel more present and give us a sense of purpose, joy and fulfilment, therefore, let your imagination go wild and have fun being creative through art, cooking, gardening, or building and designing cool things. Finding your favourite creative outlet is really important for your overall well-being and happiness.

JOY IS MY SUPER POWER

Be the joy you wish to receive

Start each day in a joyous way...

Joy is the ultimate feeling of happiness and we can find it in the things we love doing. The greatest joy is when we live our life's purpose. Helping or teaching others brings us the greatest of joy and satisfaction. So find what you love and do it often! This not only benefits others but it also fills our hearts with joy. When we experience laughter, love, and a sense of satisfaction doing what we love, these are the moments of joy that count. Taking time out to connect with the ones you love are the most joyous moments to treasure. Just by you being happy will spread joy onto others especially for your parents!

GENEROSITY IS MY SUPER POWER

Generous people feel the most joy

Start each day in a generous way...

Being generous means being really kind and caring. Generous people feel the happiest when they give to others. It is not just about big things but also small acts of kindness, like listening to others, sharing your time, and helping those who need it.

No matter how small your act of giving is, it can make a big difference. Whether you give to your loved ones or someone in need, it brings good feelings to everyone, including yourself! And guess what? When you do generous deeds, you will be rewarded in the most surprising and wonderful ways.

MY HEART IS MY SUPER POWER

Let your heart guide you

Start each day in a heartfelt way...

Imagine your heart as a magical compass that guides you on your adventures as it knows the best paths to follow and leads you toward the things you love. Your heart whispers the first tiny clues, like your gut feeling, telling you what feels right. Your head is great for thinking and protecting you but your heart is like a trusted friend you can always rely upon.

Listen to your heart and you will make the right choices to live the amazing life you were born to live. Your dreams are like wishes your heart makes so always stay true to your heart's whispers to find happiness and stay on the right path.

CONNECTION IS MY SUPER POWER

Connection raises our mood and makes us feel happy

Start each day in a connecting way...

The most joyful moments in life come from spending time with friends and family. It is all about connecting with others through listening, laughing, showing kindness and showing affection, so try and take breaks from screens and be present with your loved ones more often. When we interact with people face-to-face, we learn valuable social skills by reading their body language and facial expressions.

Human connection works like magic! It helps us thrive, grow in confidence and fills us with happiness. Spending too much time on screens or isolating ourselves from our loved ones can make us feel unmotivated, sad and lonely, however, when we find balance and connect with our community, friends, and family, our confidence grows, and we have the energy to do more of the things we love. It is good to note that socialising daily keeps our mental health in check. Remember, having a balanced life with meaningful connections is the key to happiness and well-being.

CONFIDENCE IS MY SUPER POWER
Confidence grows outside of comfort zones
Start each day in a confident way...

Confidence is something we build and not something we are born with, it grows from doing challenging things. Staying in our comfort zones might feel safe but it keeps us from becoming the best version of ourselves. When we try new things and push through uncomfortable feelings, that is when confidence starts to grow!

Do not be afraid to set achievable goals and be sure not to break any promises to yourself. This is how you learn to trust your own capabilities. Always keep learning and practicing the things you enjoy and love and that is where you will discover your unique gifts and talents and where true confidence can be found.

You must be kind to yourself, just like you would be to a friend. The way we think or speak about ourselves determines whether our dreams come true or not. Remember, confidence comes from within, and you have the power to grow it every day by affirming you CAN and you WILL achieve anything with effort.

HOPE IS MY SUPER POWER

Hope keeps us moving forward

Start each day in a hopeful way...

Having hope helps us look toward the future and it is like a magical force that makes our dreams come true and brightens even the darkest days. Every new day is like a fresh start, a chance to make wonderful things happen, so leave any worries from yesterday behind and let hope build a brighter tomorrow.

GENTLENESS IS MY SUPER POWER

Be gentle in your approach

Start each day in a gentle way...

Gentleness is all about being compassionate and kind to our emotions and feelings. When we are sensitive and gentle, it helps emotions soften and our loved ones listen to us better. The most amazing conversations happen when we listen first and respond with care.

Gentle people show strength by staying calm and thinking before they speak.

A gentle person has a heart full of love and kindness and this makes us feel safe and cared for.

PATIENCE IS MY SUPER POWER
Having patience is learning to go with the flow
Start each day in a patient way...

Having patience means letting go of control and rather being open to surprises.

When we are patient, we feel less stressed, anxious, and frustrated.

Patience is like a superpower we can learn and practice and it helps us stay calm in any situation and let go of what we expect to happen. Instead, we trust that things will work out just the way they should, at the right time.

If you ever feel impatient or upset, try taking deep breaths. Breathing exercises can help you find patience and remember, it is okay to let go of trying to control everything and rather have faith that everything will turn out just right.

INSPIRATION IS MY SUPER POWER

Inspiration is all around us

Start each day in an inspiring way...

When we see others doing things we wish to do, it can inspire us to follow our dreams too. Instead of feeling jealous or envious, be inspired to take your own steps forward. When we follow our heart's desires, our own inspiration, the right paths come to us when the time is right. Stay curious and open to what inspires you, and you will find new ideas and opportunities to fulfil your own hopes and dreams.

COMMUNICATION IS MY SUPER POWER

Communicate with gentleness

Start each day in a communicating way...

A successful conversation depends on how you speak and the way you say things. When you use gentle words, people are more likely to listen and understand you, so be kind in the way you talk to others. It is essential to communicate when you are calm and not emotional so others can really hear you.

Learning to use our words gently is like mastering a special skill and we can practice it with mindfulness. When we listen carefully, we become valuable to others and that helps conversations flow smoothly.

Remember, good communication means listening first and thinking before we speak.

NATURE IS MY SUPER POWER

Nature is our happy place

Start each day in a nature way...

Nature is a special place where you can find peace and calm. Whenever you feel overwhelmed or down, head out into nature and you will feel better. Nature's magic seems to soothe away any worries and helps you think clearly. Taking a moment to reflect, be still or even have fun exercising will always bring clarity to your thoughts.

When you are outdoors, your happy place might be the ocean, a park, or a quiet spot in the woods. Look up at the sky and you will be rewarded with beautiful clouds, sunsets, sunrises, stars, and moonlight.

Going outside in the morning or afternoon should be a promise you make to take care of your well being every day. Watching the sunrise is especially great for your gratitude practice!

Walking in nature raises your energy and changes your mood. Exercising in nature will make you feel brand new, breathe in the fresh air and exhale any stress or worries. Nature is the best healer.

MANIFESTATION IS MY SUPER POWER
Manifest your dream life
Start each day in a manifesting way...

Your imagination is like a magical door that leads to your dreams. When you visualise yourself being, doing and having all the things you wish for in your heart, anything can come true!

Instead of focusing on what you do not want, pay more attention to what you do want.

Remember, what you focus on gets all your energy. This is manifestation!

Be careful with the words you choose because you manifest what you believe. Always speak kindly about yourself and see the positive side to everything, this will give you hope and strength to get through any challenges to achieve your dreams.

Every thought you have is like a message to the universe, so dream big and keep believing in yourself. Talk about what you want to have more often so the universe can hear you.

You can have fun creating vision boards with pictures of your dream life and this will help manifest! Believe in your abilities, keep the vision in your imagination and everything will start falling into place.

LEARNING IS MY SUPER POWER

Learning grows your brain & confidence

Start each day in a learning way...

Do not be afraid of making mistakes. Mistakes are a chance to learn and grow and when we solve problems and learn from them, we become stronger and more resilient. So, do not be afraid to face your fears and try new things so you can feel capable and proud!

Did you know your brain is like a muscle? The more you exercise it, the more it will grow, therefore, do not be afraid to ask questions until you understand and that is how your confidence will grow.

Remember, trying new things is like opening a treasure chest of opportunities. Learning is not a race or competition, it is a journey that happens at your own pace, so, take your time, go slow, and enjoy the ride.

YES IS MY SUPER POWER
Say yes to life
Start each day in a yes way...

When you say YES to new opportunities and friendships you open the door to exciting adventures! YES can lead to new friends, discovering awesome things and experiencing amazing moments!

Even if you feel a bit uncomfortable, shy, or nervous, saying YES is like a superhero move to overcome those feelings. On the other side of YES, there are doors waiting to be opened and your confidence will grow like magic!

Saying no too often can keep those doors closed, rather, let the power of YES be your special key to the wonderful life you were meant to live.

NO IS MY SUPER POWER

Saying no gently is a strength

Start each day in a deciding way...

Learning to say NO gently is important when things do not feel right, it is like your heart speaking to you. Listen to your body when you feel tired or overwhelmed as it is always sending you signals.

Setting clear boundaries is taking care of yourself and it is okay to do that. Being kind to yourself helps build confidence and self-love. Remember, it is essential to take care of your own needs before helping others.

Saying NO sometimes is part of keeping your life balanced and respecting your own well-being. People who practice self-care and set boundaries are respected and valued.

READING IS MY SUPER POWER
The more you read the more you know
Start each day in a reading way...

Reading is like a delicious feast of knowledge that boosts our confidence and when we find things that interest us, reading becomes super easy and exciting!

Sharing information makes us feel smart and valuable and people who love to read are inspiring to others and hold fun and interesting conversations.

Reading is like a magical escape from worries and it helps our brain grow and learn even more.

Try starting each day by reading an uplifting affirmation or an inspiring quote. It will fill you with motivation and inspiration to make the day awesome!

UNIQUENESS IS MY SUPER POWER

Just be you

Start each day in your unique way...

Remember, the best person you can be is YOURSELF, embrace all your imperfections and quirks as they make you special and unique. True friends will not judge you, they will celebrate who you are and make you feel happy.

We all come from different backgrounds and experiences which creates our unique stories. Spend time with friends who uplift you and make you feel good about yourself.

You are born with your own special gifts and talents. Pay attention to the compliments you receive and the things you enjoy as this will lead you to your strengths and life's purpose.

When you love and accept yourself you will feel comfortable in your own skin and that confidence will shine through.

Don't waste time comparing yourself to others, just be yourself, the most authentic version of you is the most loveable.

Stay true to yourself because the world needs YOU and all your wonderful qualities so embrace who you are and you will attract the right friends who appreciate and love you for who you are.

DREAMING IS MY SUPER POWER
No dream is too big

Start each day in a dreaming way...

You were born with your very own dreams, like special wishes from your heart, so trust your heart and listen to it. Believing in yourself is like a promise you should never break and once you promise to believe in your abilities, you become unstoppable!

Dreaming gives us hope and hope keeps us looking forward to exciting things. Do not let anyone take away your sparkle, spirit, or dreams and only share your visions with those who support and uplift you.

When you do what you are passionate about, it is like finding your own kind of JOY. Hold on to this joy and it will keep you motivated to follow your dreams. Remember, dreams may take time and effort but nothing is impossible when you're determined to reach goals and hold a clear vision to your dreams.

Have faith that all happens at the right time and stay open to new opportunities along the way, because life can be even more magical than you ever dreamed.

HEALTH IS MY SUPER POWER

Be grateful for your good health

Start each day in a healthy way....

Your health is like a precious gift and every day you wake up in good health is like a miracle. Your body is like a vehicle that supports you to enjoy life to the fullest, so be grateful for all your body parts that work automatically every day, like your arms, legs, hands, feet, eyes, and ears.

Your strong heart beating keeps your whole body going so it is important to take care of it. Healthy food choices are like super fuel for your mind and body, similar to fuel that keeps a car running. Fill your body with goodness and nutrients to stay active and full of energy.

Moving your body every day with exercise is essential for feeling your best, and it is even more fun when you exercise in nature. Eating more fresh foods from the land and trees and less processed ones gives you lots of energy!

Being kind to your body and taking care of it is self-love, so remember to give thanks to your good health every day.

SMILING IS MY SUPER POWER
Smiles are contagious and kind
Start each day in a smiling way...

Smiles are like magic! When you meet someone for the first time, they notice your smile, and it tells them so much about you. A smile brings instant connection and shows that you are kind and confident. Always wear your beautiful smile to make people feel comfortable and welcomed.

Remember, smiles are contagious and spread happiness and kindness and your smile can brighten someone's tough day and make them feel noticed, loved, and connected. Keep shining your kind self with your loving, bright smile.

HONESTY IS MY SUPER POWER

Honest people have nothing to hide

Start each day in a honest way...

Honesty is like a badge of trust and when you always tell the truth you don't have to worry about getting your story wrong. Honest people sleep well at night because they have nothing to hide. Being honest with yourself and others makes you trustworthy, admired, and respected. So, never tell a lie because it usually comes back to you.

When you stay true to your core values and always choose honesty, you attract the right people into your life.

LAUGHING IS MY SUPER POWER

Laughing brings us the ultimate of joy

Start each day in a laughing way...

Laughing is like a burst of joy that fills our hearts with happiness and when we laugh out loud, it is the greatest feeling ever!

Laughing is like magic as it helps us release stress and makes tough times easier to handle. Try to find the funny side in everything, and make laughing a part of your daily routine with friends and family. It is a wonderful way to connect and create great memories together.

Having a great sense of humour is like a super spreader of happiness! People love it and laughter is contagious. When we laugh, it releases feel-good endorphins that keep us healthy and happy, so let's keep laughing and spreading joy.

CELEBRATING IS MY SUPER POWER

Celebrate small and big things

Start each day in a celebratory way...

Special occasions are like magical moments that fill our hearts with joy and create treasured memories. Instead of worrying about getting older, let's celebrate the blessing of another birthday! Not everyone gets to live another year, so it is something truly special.

Celebrating is also about embracing all of our wins, big or small and every challenge we overcome is a win and we should pat ourselves on the back for all our achievements, whether it is school tasks, projects, or personal lessons, each one is a step towards growing stronger and more resilient. Show appreciation for every milestone you reach and inspire others to celebrate their achievements too!

Remember, loving ourselves means celebrating the person we've become and the adversity we've overcome. Life is a precious gift, and every moment is worth celebrating and appreciating.

FAITH IS MY SUPER POWER

Have faith and the rest will fall into place

Start each day in a faithful way...

Having faith is like having a superpower that can do amazing things! Believe in all the wonderful things you were born to achieve and have confidence in your special gifts, talents, and dreams. Every day give thanks to the universe, God, or whatever higher power you believe in.

Having faith gives us peace during tough times and brings hope and guidance when you need it. Sometimes, it's good to let go of control and trust that things will work out just right.

If things don't go smoothly, have faith that maybe it is not the right time yet. When you lean on faith, easier paths may open up to you, so stay open to signs guiding you along your journey, and you may find little hints and messages to follow.

When you give thanks every day for the blessings you have, amazing things start to happen. Have faith and stay grateful and everything will fall into place.

I am so pleased you found this book and for good reason too, as it is my belief that we are all here to learn and grow into the best versions of ourselves.

This latest book is from my life experiences and observations. I lived a charmed life modelling, travelling the world and living life to the full but then my world turned upside down when my mother passed and my marriage ended at the same time. Dealing with the grief of loss and needing the strength to raise my three-year-old as a single parent, I turned to healing practices; mindfulness, creativity, gratitude and positivity which was inspired by my psychology research, thought leaders and life coaches.

On my path to healing, I discovered painting art and this book is a combination of my love of art and positive psychology. My Boathouse Studio on the Northern Beaches of Sydney has provided an inspiring space for me to teach art and create helpful resources using all the wisdom I have gained along my journey.

I hope this little book can help you along your path...

Kylie
♡ xx